The Real Estate Market 101 Secrets to Success

Overview:

The real estate market is one of the most lucrative and dynamic industries in the world. With the potential for high returns and the ability to create wealth, it's no wonder that many people are drawn to real estate investing. However, the market can also be unpredictable and challenging for beginners, making it difficult to achieve success. In this comprehensive guide, real estate expert John Smith shares his wealth of knowledge and experience to provide readers with the secrets to success in the real estate market. Whether you're a novice investor or a seasoned professional, this book will help you navigate the complexities of the market and achieve your goals.

Table of Contents:

Chapter 1: Introduction to Real Estate Investing
- Why invest in real estate?
- Types of real estate investments
- Risks and benefits of real estate investing

Chapter 2: Market Analysis
- Understanding the real estate market
- Conducting a market analysis
- Identifying market trends and opportunities

Chapter 3: Financing
- Financing options for real estate investments
- Evaluating financing options
- Managing financing risks

Chapter 4: Property Acquisition
- Finding and evaluating properties
- Negotiating deals
- Due diligence and closing

Chapter 5: Property Management
- Responsibilities of a property manager
- Choosing a property management strategy
- Handling tenant issues and maintenance

Chapter 6: Marketing and Selling
- Developing a marketing strategy
- Preparing a property for sale
- Negotiating and closing a sale

Chapter 7: Taxation and Legal Considerations
- Tax implications of real estate investments
- Legal considerations for real estate transactions
- Minimizing legal and tax risks

Chapter 8: Real Estate Investment Strategies
- Buy and hold
- Flipping properties
- REITs and other investment vehicles

Chapter 9: Real Estate Market Trends and Forecast
- Emerging trends in the real estate market
- Predictions for the future of the market
- How to stay ahead of the curve

Chapter 10: Conclusion and Next Steps

- Review of key concepts
- Actionable steps for success

Chapter 1: Introduction to Real Estate Investing

Real estate investing is the purchase, ownership, management, rental, and/or sale of real estate for profit. It can be a lucrative and rewarding industry for those who understand the market and have a solid investment strategy. This chapter will provide an overview of real estate investing, including its benefits and risks, types of real estate investments, and factors to consider when deciding whether to invest in real estate.

Why Invest in Real Estate? Real estate has long been considered one of the best ways to build wealth and create a steady income stream. There are several reasons why real estate investing is so attractive:

1. Tangible Asset: Real estate is a tangible asset that you can touch, feel, and see. This makes it less volatile than other investments such as stocks and bonds, which can be impacted by factors such as market conditions, economic downturns, and geopolitical events.

2. Cash Flow: Real estate provides an opportunity for cash flow through rental income. This can be particularly beneficial for investors who are looking for a passive income stream to supplement their other sources of income.

3. Appreciation: Real estate has the potential for long-term appreciation, which can result in significant returns over time. Historically, real estate has appreciated at a rate of around 3-4% per year, which is comparable to the rate of inflation.

4. Tax Benefits: Real estate investors can take advantage of several tax benefits, including depreciation, mortgage interest deductions, and property tax deductions. These tax benefits

can significantly reduce the amount of taxes that investors are required to pay.

Types of Real Estate Investments: There are several types of real estate investments, each with its own set of benefits and risks. Here are some of the most common types of real estate investments:

1. Residential Real Estate: Residential real estate includes single-family homes, duplexes, triplexes, and apartments. These properties are generally used for residential purposes, such as living quarters for tenants. Residential real estate is often considered a good starting point for new investors, as it is more accessible and easier to understand than other types of real estate investments.

2. Commercial Real Estate: Commercial real estate includes office buildings, retail spaces, warehouses, and other properties that are used for commercial purposes. These properties are often larger and more complex than residential properties, and they typically require more capital to invest in. However, commercial real estate can offer higher returns than residential properties, especially for investors who are willing to take on more risk.

3. Industrial Real Estate: Industrial real estate includes properties that are used for manufacturing, distribution, and other industrial purposes. These properties are often located in industrial parks or other areas that are zoned for industrial use. Industrial real estate can be a good investment for investors who are looking for long-term, stable returns.

4. Raw Land: Raw land refers to undeveloped land that is not currently being used for any purpose. This type of real estate investment can be risky, as there are no structures or tenants to generate income. However, raw land can also offer significant upside potential if it is located in an area that is expected to experience growth in the future.

Risks and Benefits of Real Estate Investing: While real estate investing can be a great way to build wealth and create a passive income stream, it is not without its risks. Here are some of the benefits and risks of real estate investing:

Benefits:

- Tangible Asset: Real estate is a tangible asset that you can see, touch, and feel. This can provide a sense of security and stability that other types of investments may not offer.

- Passive Income: Real estate can provide a passive income stream through rental income. This can be a great way to supplement your other sources of income and create financial stability.

- Appreciation: Real estate has the potential for long-term appreciation, which can result in significant returns over time. This appreciation can come from market forces or through improvements to the property itself.

- Tax Benefits: Real estate investors can take advantage of several tax benefits, including depreciation, mortgage interest deductions, and property tax deductions. These tax benefits can significantly reduce the amount of taxes that investors are required to pay.

Risks:

- Market Fluctuations: Real estate markets can be volatile, and market fluctuations can impact the value of your investment. Economic downturns or changes in interest rates can negatively impact the value of your investment.

- Property Management: Managing a property can be time-consuming and expensive, especially if you are not experienced in property management. If you hire a property manager, this can eat into your profits.

- Vacancies: If you rely on rental income, vacancies can be a significant risk to your investment. If you cannot find tenants to occupy your property, you may have to cover the costs of the property yourself.
- Unexpected Expenses: Real estate investments can come with unexpected expenses, such as repairs, renovations, and maintenance costs. These expenses can significantly impact your profitability.

Factors to Consider When Deciding Whether to Invest in Real Estate: Before investing in real estate, there are several factors to consider. Here are some of the most important factors to keep in mind:

1. Investment Goals: Your investment goals will play a significant role in determining whether real estate investing is right for you. If you are looking for long-term appreciation and passive income, real estate may be a good investment. However, if you are looking for short-term gains, stocks or other investments may be more appropriate.
2. Risk Tolerance: Real estate investing can be risky, and you need to have a high level of risk tolerance to be successful in this industry. If you are risk-averse, real estate may not be the right investment for you.
3. Market Conditions: The real estate market is influenced by various market conditions, such as interest rates, economic conditions, and population growth. Before investing in real estate, you need to research market conditions in your desired location to ensure that your investment is likely to appreciate in value.
4. Financing: Real estate investing requires a significant amount of capital, and you may need to obtain financing to purchase a property. Before investing in real estate, you need to understand the various

financing options available to you and determine which one is the best fit for your investment goals.

Conclusion: Real estate investing can be a lucrative and rewarding industry for those who understand the market and have a solid investment strategy. However, real estate investing is not without its risks, and it requires a significant amount of research and due diligence to be successful. By understanding the benefits and risks of real estate investing, and by carefully considering the various factors that influence real estate investments, you can make informed decisions and build a successful real estate investment portfolio.

Chapter 2: Understanding the Real Estate Market

The real estate market is a complex and dynamic industry that is influenced by a wide range of factors, including economic conditions, interest rates, and demographic trends. Understanding the real estate market is critical to making informed investment decisions and building a successful real estate portfolio. In this chapter, we will discuss the key components of the real estate market and how they impact the value of real estate investments.

The Real Estate Market The real estate market is a broad term that refers to the buying and selling of real estate properties. The market is composed of several sub-markets, including residential, commercial, industrial, and agricultural markets. Each sub-market has unique characteristics and is influenced by different factors.

The residential market is the most active sub-market and includes properties that are used for residential purposes, such as single-family homes, townhouses, and apartments. The commercial market includes properties that are used for business purposes, such as office buildings, retail stores, and warehouses. The industrial market includes properties that are used for manufacturing and production, such as factories and distribution centers. The agricultural market includes properties that are used for farming and agriculture.

Market Factors The real estate market is influenced by a wide range of factors, including economic conditions, interest rates, and demographic trends. Understanding these factors is critical to making informed investment decisions.

Economic Conditions The real estate market is closely tied to economic conditions. In general, when the economy is strong, the real estate market tends to perform well. Economic growth leads to increased job opportunities, which in turn leads to increased demand for housing and commercial properties. When the economy is weak, however, the real estate market tends to struggle.

Interest Rates Interest rates also play a critical role in the real estate market. When interest rates are low, it is cheaper to borrow money, which can lead to increased demand for real estate. Low interest rates can also increase the affordability of mortgages, making it easier for people to purchase homes. When interest rates are high, however, borrowing becomes more expensive, which can lead to decreased demand for real estate.

Demographic Trends Demographic trends can also impact the real estate market. Changes in population size and demographics can lead to changes in demand for certain types of properties. For example, an increase in the number of young professionals in a particular area may lead to increased demand for rental properties and condominiums.

Market Cycles The real estate market is cyclical and experiences periods of growth and decline. These cycles are influenced by a variety of factors, including economic conditions, interest rates, and demographic trends. Understanding market cycles is critical to making informed investment decisions.

During a period of growth, demand for real estate is high, and property values tend to appreciate. During a period of decline, demand for real estate is low, and property values tend to decline. It is important to note that market cycles vary by location and property type. For example, the residential market may experience a different cycle than the commercial market.

Real Estate Metrics There are several metrics that real estate investors use to evaluate the performance of a property. These metrics can help investors determine whether a property is a good investment opportunity.

Cash Flow Cash flow refers to the amount of money that a property generates after all expenses have been paid. Positive cash flow is a key indicator of a good investment opportunity, as it means that the property is generating more income than it costs to operate.

Appreciation refers to the increase in value of a property over time. Properties that appreciate in value can provide significant returns to investors, especially if the property is held for a long period of time.

Cap Rate The capitalization rate, or cap rate, is a metric used to evaluate the return on investment for a property. The cap rate is calculated by dividing the property's net operating income (NOI) by its market value. A higher cap rate indicates a higher return on investment.

Leverage refers to the use of borrowed money to purchase a property. Leveraging can increase the potential return on investment, but it also increases the risk. It is important for investors to carefully evaluate the risks and benefits of leveraging before making a purchase.

Market Analysis Before investing in a property, it is important to conduct a thorough market analysis to evaluate the potential risks and rewards. A market analysis should consider factors such as the local economy, population demographics, and property values.

Location is also a critical factor in real estate investment. Properties located in desirable neighborhoods with access to transportation and amenities tend to perform well in the market. Properties in less desirable neighborhoods may be cheaper to purchase but may also be riskier investments.

In addition to location, it is important to consider the property's condition, age, and potential for renovation or improvement. Properties that require significant repairs or improvements may be cheaper to purchase, but may also require significant investment to bring up to market standards.

Conclusion Understanding the real estate market is critical to making informed investment decisions and building a successful real estate portfolio. The real estate market is influenced by a wide range of factors, including economic conditions, interest rates, and demographic trends. By carefully evaluating these factors and conducting a thorough market analysis, investors can identify potential investment opportunities and build a profitable real estate portfolio. In the next chapter, we will discuss the different types of real estate investments and their respective advantages and disadvantages.

Chapter 3: Types of Real Estate Investments

Real estate investments come in many forms, each with its own unique set of advantages and disadvantages. In this chapter, we will explore the most common types of real estate investments and discuss their respective pros and cons.

1. Single-Family Homes Single-family homes are the most common type of real estate investment. They are relatively easy to acquire and manage, making them a popular choice for new investors. Single-family homes can generate steady rental income and appreciate in value over time. However, they also come with their own set of challenges, including the need to deal with tenants and maintenance issues.

2. Multi-Family Properties Multi-family properties, such as apartment buildings or townhouses, are another popular type of real estate investment. They can provide a steady stream of rental income and allow investors to scale their investments by acquiring multiple units within a single property. Multi-family properties also offer some economies of scale when it comes to maintenance and management. However, they can be more complex to manage than single-family homes and may require more upfront investment.

3. Commercial Real Estate Commercial real estate includes properties used for commercial purposes, such as office buildings, retail spaces, and warehouses. Commercial real estate investments can offer higher returns than residential properties, but they also come with greater risks. For example, commercial tenants may be more likely to default on their lease payments during economic downturns, and vacancies can be harder to fill. Additionally, commercial

properties often require higher upfront investment and more complex management.

4. Real Estate Investment Trusts (REITs) A real estate investment trust (REIT) is a type of investment that pools money from multiple investors to purchase and manage real estate assets. REITs offer investors a way to invest in real estate without the need to manage properties directly. They can provide regular income and capital appreciation, but they also come with fees and other costs that can eat into returns.

5. Real Estate Crowdfunding Real estate crowdfunding is a relatively new type of investment that allows investors to pool their money to purchase and manage real estate assets. Crowdfunding platforms often offer investments in commercial or residential properties, and investors can typically invest with relatively small amounts of money. Real estate crowdfunding can offer investors the potential for high returns, but it also comes with risks, including the potential for fraudulent or poorly managed projects.

6. Fix-and-Flip Properties Fix-and-flip properties are residential properties that investors purchase with the intention of renovating and selling for a profit. This strategy can generate significant returns if executed correctly, but it also comes with significant risks. Investors must accurately assess the costs of repairs and renovations, and they must be able to sell the property for a profit once the work is complete.

Conclusion Real estate investments come in many forms, each with its own unique set of advantages and disadvantages. Single-family homes and multi-family properties are popular choices for new investors, while commercial real estate can offer higher returns for experienced investors. Real estate investment trusts and crowdfunding platforms offer ways to invest in real estate without the need to manage properties directly, while fix-and-flip properties can offer significant returns for investors with the right skills and experience. By understanding the different types of real estate investments and their respective risks and rewards, investors can make informed investment decisions and build a successful real estate portfolio.

Chapter 4: Financing Real Estate Investments

Financing is a critical aspect of real estate investment. Most investors rely on financing to purchase properties, and understanding the different financing options available is essential for building a successful real estate portfolio. In this chapter, we will explore the most common financing options for real estate investments and discuss their respective advantages and disadvantages.

1. Conventional Mortgages Conventional mortgages are the most common type of financing for residential real estate investments. They are offered by banks and other financial institutions and typically require a down payment of 20% or more. Conventional mortgages offer competitive interest rates and terms, but they also come with strict eligibility requirements, including a good credit score and stable income.

2. FHA Loans FHA loans are government-backed loans that are designed to help first-time homebuyers and low-income borrowers purchase homes. They require a lower down payment than conventional mortgages, typically around 3.5%, and have more relaxed eligibility requirements. However, FHA loans also come with additional fees and requirements, including mortgage insurance premiums and stricter property appraisal standards.

3. Hard Money Loans Hard money loans are short-term loans that are secured by the value of the property being purchased. They are typically offered by private lenders and have higher interest rates and fees than conventional mortgages. Hard money loans are often used by investors who need to close

on a property quickly or who are unable to qualify for a conventional mortgage.

4. Seller Financing Seller financing is a type of financing where the seller of the property provides the financing for the buyer. This can be an attractive option for investors who are unable to secure conventional financing or who want to negotiate more flexible terms. However, seller financing can also be risky, as the terms may be less favorable than conventional financing, and the seller may not have the financial stability to provide the financing.

5. Private Equity Private equity is a type of financing where investors pool their money together to purchase and manage real estate assets. Private equity investments can offer higher returns than other financing options, but they also come with higher risks. Investors must have a high net worth and significant experience in real estate investments to participate in private equity deals.

6. Crowdfunding Real estate crowdfunding platforms can also offer financing options for real estate investments. Crowdfunding platforms allow investors to pool their money together to finance a real estate project, and investors typically receive a share of the profits generated by the project. Crowdfunding can offer lower investment minimums and more flexible terms than other financing options, but it also comes with higher fees and risks.

Conclusion Financing is a critical aspect of real estate investment, and understanding the different financing options available is essential for building a successful real estate portfolio. Conventional mortgages and FHA loans are common options for residential real estate investments, while hard money loans and seller financing may be better options for investors who need more flexible terms. Private equity and crowdfunding can offer higher returns but come with higher risks. By understanding the advantages and disadvantages of each financing option, investors can make informed decisions and build a successful real estate portfolio. In the next chapter, we will discuss the importance of due diligence in real estate investments.

Chapter 5: Due Diligence in Real Estate Investments

Due diligence is a critical aspect of real estate investing that involves conducting thorough research and analysis of a property before making an investment decision. By conducting due diligence, investors can assess the risks and potential returns of a real estate investment and make informed decisions. In this chapter, we will explore the key components of due diligence in real estate investments and discuss their importance.

1. Property Inspection Property inspection is a crucial component of due diligence in real estate investments. A property inspection involves hiring a licensed inspector to evaluate the condition of the property and identify any potential issues or defects. This includes assessing the foundation, roof, plumbing, electrical, and HVAC systems, as well as any visible signs of damage or wear and tear. A property inspection can help investors identify potential repair costs and negotiate a fair purchase price.

2. Title Search A title search is another critical component of due diligence in real estate investments. A title search involves hiring a title company to review the property's title history and ensure that the seller has the legal right to sell the property. This includes checking for any liens, encumbrances, or other legal issues that could prevent the sale of the property. A title search can help investors avoid costly legal disputes and ensure that they have clear ownership of the property.

3. Market Analysis Market analysis is an essential component of due diligence in real estate investments. A market analysis

involves evaluating the local real estate market and assessing the supply and demand for properties in the area. This includes evaluating the current market conditions, analyzing recent sales data, and assessing the potential for future growth or decline in the market. A market analysis can help investors identify properties that are priced below market value or located in high-growth areas.

4. Financial Analysis Financial analysis is another critical component of due diligence in real estate investments. A financial analysis involves evaluating the financial performance of the property, including the potential rental income, expenses, and cash flow. This includes analyzing the property's income and expense statements, calculating the potential return on investment (ROI), and assessing the property's overall profitability. A financial analysis can help investors determine whether a property is a sound investment and identify potential areas for improvement.

5. Zoning and Permitting Zoning and permitting are important considerations in real estate investments, particularly for commercial or multifamily properties. Zoning regulations and permits can impact the property's use, development potential, and value. Investors should research the local zoning and permitting regulations and assess any potential restrictions or requirements that could impact the property's use or development potential.

6. Environmental Assessment Environmental assessment is another important component of due diligence in real estate investments. An environmental assessment involves evaluating the property's environmental condition and identifying any potential environmental hazards or liabilities. This includes assessing the presence of hazardous materials, evaluating the property's compliance with environmental regulations, and identifying any potential environmental risks or liabilities. An environmental assessment can help investors

avoid potential legal and financial liabilities and ensure that the property is safe for tenants and occupants.

Conclusion Due diligence is a critical aspect of real estate investing, and conducting thorough research and analysis is essential for making informed investment decisions. Property inspection, title search, market analysis, financial analysis, zoning and permitting, and environmental assessment are key components of due diligence in real estate investments. By conducting due diligence, investors can assess the risks and potential returns of a real estate investment and make informed decisions. In the next chapter, we will discuss the importance of property management in real estate investments.

Chapter 6: Property Management in Real Estate Investments

Property management is a critical aspect of real estate investing that involves the management and operation of a property to ensure its long-term profitability and success. A property manager is responsible for handling day-to-day tasks such as tenant screening, rent collection, maintenance, and repairs. In this chapter, we will explore the importance of property management in real estate investments and discuss the key considerations for successful property management.

1. Tenant Screening One of the primary responsibilities of a property manager is tenant screening. Tenant screening involves evaluating potential tenants' credit history, rental history, and employment status to ensure that they are responsible and reliable renters. A property manager should also conduct a background check to assess any potential criminal history. Tenant screening is critical for minimizing the risk of late payments, evictions, and property damage.

2. Rent Collection Rent collection is another critical aspect of property management in real estate investments. A property manager should have a clear and consistent rent collection policy to ensure timely payments from tenants. This includes setting clear due dates, sending reminders, and enforcing late fees for missed payments. A property manager should also be prepared to handle any rent disputes or evictions promptly and effectively.

3. Maintenance and Repairs Maintenance and repairs are essential components of successful property management in real estate investments. A property manager should conduct regular inspections to identify any necessary repairs or

maintenance tasks, such as painting, landscaping, or cleaning. They should also handle emergency repairs promptly to prevent further damage and ensure tenant safety. A property manager should maintain a network of reliable contractors and vendors to ensure high-quality work and cost-effective services.

4. Budgeting and Financial Management Budgeting and financial management are important considerations for property management in real estate investments. A property manager should maintain accurate and up-to-date records of all income and expenses, including rent payments, maintenance costs, and property taxes. They should also develop a comprehensive budget and financial plan to ensure the property's long-term profitability and success. This includes identifying potential cost savings, maximizing rental income, and forecasting future expenses.

5. Tenant Relations Tenant relations are critical for successful property management in real estate investments. A property manager should maintain open and transparent communication with tenants, responding promptly to any questions or concerns. They should also foster positive tenant relations by organizing community events and addressing any complaints or disputes promptly and professionally. Building strong tenant relationships can help to minimize tenant turnover and increase tenant satisfaction.

6. Legal Compliance Legal compliance is another important consideration for property management in real estate investments. A property manager should be familiar with all local and state regulations related to landlord-tenant relationships, fair housing, and other legal considerations. They should also be prepared to handle any legal disputes or issues promptly and effectively, working closely with legal counsel if necessary.

Conclusion Property management is a critical aspect of real estate investing, and successful property management requires careful planning, attention to detail, and a focus on tenant satisfaction. Tenant screening, rent collection, maintenance and repairs, budgeting and financial management, tenant relations, and legal compliance are all key considerations for successful property management in real estate investments. By prioritizing these key components, investors can maximize their returns and ensure the long-term success of their real estate investments. In the next chapter, we will discuss the importance of networking and building relationships in real estate investing.

Chapter 7: Networking and Building Relationships in Real Estate Investing

Networking and building relationships are critical components of success in real estate investing. As an investor, you will need to establish relationships with a wide range of individuals and organizations, including other investors, real estate agents, lenders, contractors, and property managers. In this chapter, we will explore the importance of networking and building relationships in real estate investing and discuss the key strategies for building a successful network.

1. Why Networking is Important in Real Estate Investing
   Networking is critical for success in real estate investing for several reasons. First, networking allows you to connect with other investors and professionals in the industry, allowing you to share knowledge, resources, and best practices. This can help you to identify new investment opportunities, access financing and funding, and overcome challenges and obstacles. Second, networking helps you to establish a reputation and build credibility in the industry, which can help you to attract partners, clients, and opportunities.

2. Key Strategies for Networking in Real Estate Investing There are several key strategies for networking in real estate investing, including:

- Attend industry events: Attending industry events such as real estate conferences, networking events, and seminars can provide valuable opportunities to meet and connect with other investors and professionals in the industry. Be sure to bring plenty of business cards and be prepared to introduce yourself and your business.

- Join local real estate groups: Joining local real estate groups such as real estate investing associations and clubs can help you to build relationships with other investors in your area. These groups often host meetings, events, and educational opportunities for members.

- Connect with real estate agents: Real estate agents can be valuable partners and resources for real estate investors, as they often have access to off-market deals and can provide valuable insights into local market trends and conditions.

- Build relationships with lenders and financing professionals: Building relationships with lenders and financing professionals can help you to access funding and financing for your real estate investments. Consider reaching out to local banks, credit unions, and private lenders to explore financing options.

- Establish relationships with contractors and property managers: Establishing relationships with reliable contractors and property managers can help you to ensure that your properties are well-maintained and managed, reducing the risk of property damage and tenant turnover.

3. Building Credibility and Reputation in Real Estate Investing
Building credibility and reputation in real estate investing is critical for attracting partners, clients, and opportunities. There are several key strategies for building credibility and reputation in real estate investing, including:

- Focus on quality and integrity: Focus on providing high-quality investments and services, and operate with integrity and honesty in all of your business dealings.

- Build a strong online presence: Establish a professional website and social media presence, and regularly share valuable content and insights related to real estate investing.

- Ask for testimonials and referrals: Ask satisfied clients and partners for testimonials and referrals, and use these to build your reputation and credibility.

- Attend educational and professional development opportunities: Attend real estate investing courses, seminars, and other educational opportunities to build your knowledge and expertise in the industry.

4. Leveraging Technology and Tools for Networking and Building Relationships Leveraging technology and tools can help you to streamline your networking and relationship-building efforts in real estate investing. Some useful tools and resources include:

- Real estate investing software: Real estate investing software can help you to manage your investments, analyze market trends, and track your progress towards your goals.

- CRM software: Customer relationship management (CRM) software can help you to manage and track your relationships with partners, clients, and vendors.

- Online networking platforms: Online networking platforms such as LinkedIn and Bigger Pockets can provide valuable opportunities to connect with other investors and professionals in the industry.

Conclusion Networking and building relationships are critical components of success in real estate investing. By leveraging the strategies and tools outlined in this chapter, you can establish a strong network and build a reputation as a credible and reliable real estate investor. Remember to focus on quality, integrity, and professionalism in all of your business dealings, and to regularly invest in your own education and professional development.

By attending industry events, joining local real estate groups, connecting with real estate agents, building relationships with lenders and financing professionals, and establishing relationships with contractors and property managers, you can expand your network and gain access to new investment opportunities and resources.

In addition, by leveraging technology and tools such as real estate investing software, CRM software, and online networking platforms, you can streamline your networking and relationship-building efforts, making it easier to stay organized and connected with your partners, clients, and vendors.

Ultimately, building a strong network and reputation in real estate investing requires a commitment to excellence, integrity, and ongoing learning and development. By prioritizing these values and strategies, you can establish yourself as a trusted and successful real estate investor, and achieve long-term success and growth in this exciting and dynamic industry.

Chapter 8: Mitigating Risks in Real Estate Investing

Real estate investing can be a profitable and rewarding business, but like any investment, it also carries a degree of risk. Fortunately, there are several strategies and tools that investors can use to mitigate these risks and protect their investments.

1. Conducting thorough due diligence

   One of the most important ways to mitigate risk in real estate investing is by conducting thorough due diligence on every potential investment opportunity. This means doing your homework and gathering as much information as possible about the property, the local real estate market, and the surrounding neighborhood.

   Some key due diligence steps to take include:

   - Conducting a property inspection to identify any structural or maintenance issues
   - Reviewing the property's financial statements and rent roll
   - Evaluating the local real estate market to determine whether the property is located in an area with strong demand and growth potential
   - Researching the neighborhood to identify any potential risks or issues that could affect property values or rental income.

2. Diversifying your portfolio

   Another key strategy for mitigating risk in real estate investing is to diversify your portfolio. Rather than putting all of your eggs in one basket, consider investing in a range of properties, locations, and asset classes, such as residential, commercial, and industrial properties.

Diversification can help protect your investments by spreading your risk across a range of different assets and markets, reducing your exposure to any single property or location.

3. Maintaining adequate insurance coverage

   Insurance is an essential tool for mitigating risk in real estate investing. As a property owner, you should carry adequate insurance coverage to protect your investment against risks such as fire, theft, and liability claims.

   Some types of insurance coverage to consider include:

   - Property insurance, which covers damage to the physical structure and any personal property within the building

   - Liability insurance, which protects against claims of injury or property damage caused by the property

   - Flood insurance, which covers damage from floods or other water-related events.

4. Understanding and complying with regulations

   Real estate investing is subject to a range of laws and regulations, including zoning laws, building codes, and landlord-tenant laws. As an investor, it's important to understand these regulations and comply with them to avoid legal risks and potential penalties.

   Working with an experienced attorney or real estate professional can help ensure that you understand and comply with all applicable regulations and laws.

5. Staying up-to-date on market trends

Staying up-to-date on market trends and conditions is another important way to mitigate risk in real estate investing. By keeping a close eye on market trends, you can identify potential risks and opportunities and adjust your investment strategy accordingly.

Some key market trends to monitor include:

- Supply and demand dynamics in your local market
- Economic and demographic trends that could affect property values and rental demand
- Interest rate fluctuations that could affect financing costs and investment returns.

6. Building a strong team

    Building a strong team of professionals, including real estate agents, attorneys, property managers, and contractors, can help you mitigate risk in real estate investing. These professionals can provide valuable expertise, advice, and support throughout the investment process, helping you identify and address potential risks and issues.

    When building your team, look for professionals with a track record of success in your local market, and consider their experience and expertise in your specific asset class or investment strategy.

7. Maintaining adequate reserves

    Finally, maintaining adequate reserves is an important strategy for mitigating risk in real estate investing. By setting aside funds for unexpected expenses, such as repairs, maintenance, and vacancies, you can avoid cash flow issues and protect your investment against unexpected events.

As a general rule, it's a good idea to maintain reserves equal to at least six months of expenses for each property in your portfolio.

In summary , real estate investing can be a lucrative and rewarding business, but it's important to understand and mitigate the risks involved. By conducting thorough due diligence, diversifying your portfolio, maintaining adequate insurance coverage, understanding and complying with regulations, staying up-to-date on market trends, building a strong team, and maintaining adequate reserves, you can protect your investments and increase your chances of success.

Remember, real estate investing is a long-term game, and success requires patience, persistence, and a willingness to learn and adapt. By taking the time to understand the risks and implement strategies to mitigate them, you can build a profitable and sustainable real estate investment portfolio.

Chapter 9: Building Your Real Estate Investment Team

Real estate investing is not a one-person job. It requires a team of professionals to help you navigate the complex world of real estate transactions and investments. Building a solid team can be the difference between success and failure in real estate investing. In this chapter, we will discuss the various professionals you need on your team, their roles, and how to find and work with them.

1. Real Estate Agent A real estate agent is your go-to professional for buying and selling properties. They are licensed professionals who can help you identify and analyze potential investment properties, negotiate deals, and navigate the buying and selling process. A good agent can also connect you with other professionals such as attorneys, inspectors, and lenders.

   When choosing a real estate agent, look for someone with experience and knowledge of the local market. They should also have a strong track record of successful transactions and positive reviews from previous clients. You should feel comfortable communicating with them and trust their advice.

2. Real Estate Attorney A real estate attorney is an important part of your team, especially when it comes to complex transactions such as commercial real estate or multi-unit properties. They can review contracts, handle legal disputes, and ensure that your investments are legally protected. A good attorney should have experience in real estate law and be familiar with the local regulations and zoning laws.

   When choosing a real estate attorney, look for someone with experience in the specific type of transaction you are working on. They should have a strong understanding of the legal and regulatory requirements of the local market.

3. Real Estate Accountant A real estate accountant can help you manage your finances and ensure that your investments are profitable. They can help you with tax planning, bookkeeping, financial analysis, and creating investment strategies. They can also help you identify areas where you can save money and increase your profits.

    When choosing a real estate accountant, look for someone with experience in real estate investing. They should be familiar with the tax implications of different types of investments and have a strong understanding of real estate accounting.

4. Property Inspector A property inspector can help you identify potential issues with a property before you purchase it. They can identify problems such as structural issues, mold, pest infestations, and other issues that can affect the value of the property. They can also provide a detailed report of their findings, which can help you negotiate the price or make an informed decision about whether to proceed with the purchase.

    When choosing a property inspector, look for someone with experience in the specific type of property you are interested in. They should be licensed and insured and have a strong reputation for providing accurate and thorough inspections.

5. Property Manager A property manager can help you manage your rental properties and ensure that they are profitable. They can handle tasks such as tenant screening, rent collection, maintenance and repairs, and dealing with tenant issues. They can also help you identify ways to increase your profits, such as raising rents or reducing expenses.

    When choosing a property manager, look for someone with experience in managing properties similar to yours. They should be licensed and insured and have a strong track record of managing properties efficiently and effectively.

6. Lender A lender can provide financing for your real estate investments. They can help you find the best loan options for your needs and ensure that you have the funding you need to complete your transactions. They can also provide advice on how to structure your deals to minimize your risks and maximize your profits.

   When choosing a lender, look for someone with experience in real estate financing. They should be able to provide a range of loan options and be willing to work with you to find the best solution for your needs.

7. Contractor A contractor can help you manage renovations and repairs on your properties. They can handle tasks such as painting,

   After considering all the factors and analyzing the property, it's time to make an offer. This is the most critical step in the process, as it can make or break the entire deal. Here are some things to keep in mind when making an offer:

   1. Be realistic: Your offer should be based on the property's value, not your budget or what you think it should be worth. It's crucial to stay within your means and not overpay for a property, as this can lead to financial strain and even failure.
   2. Know the market: Understanding the real estate market is essential when making an offer. Research similar properties in the area and how much they have sold for. This will help you determine a fair offer and negotiate effectively.
   3. Don't be afraid to negotiate: The seller may not accept your first offer, and that's okay. Negotiation is a standard part of the buying process, so don't be afraid

to counteroffer or walk away if the seller isn't willing to budge.
4. Consider contingencies: Contingencies are clauses in the contract that protect you in case of unforeseen circumstances, such as inspection issues or financing problems. Be sure to include contingencies in your offer, but don't go overboard, as too many contingencies can deter the seller from accepting.
5. Be prepared: Before making an offer, ensure you have all your finances in order and a pre-approval letter from your lender. This shows the seller that you are serious about the purchase and have the means to close the deal.
6. Hire a real estate attorney: Having a real estate attorney review and negotiate the contract can provide an extra layer of protection and ensure that all legal requirements are met.

Once the offer is made, it's a waiting game to hear back from the seller. If the offer is accepted, congratulations! The next step is to move forward with the closing process. If the offer is declined or countered, don't be discouraged. It's common for offers to go back and forth before an agreement is reached.

In conclusion, making an offer is a critical step in the real estate buying process. It's essential to be realistic, know the market, and negotiate effectively. With proper preparation and the right mindset, you can make an offer that is fair for both you and the seller.

Chapter 10: Tips for Success in the Real Estate Market

Now that you have learned about the different aspects of the real estate market and how to invest in it, here are some tips to help you succeed in this industry.

1. Keep Learning and Stay Updated: The real estate market is constantly changing, and it is crucial to stay updated on the latest trends and regulations. Attend workshops, seminars, and training programs, and read books and articles related to real estate investing. Stay connected with other real estate investors and professionals to gain insights and knowledge.

2. Develop a Business Plan: Create a clear and concise business plan that outlines your goals, strategies, and timeline. This will help you stay focused and track your progress. It will also help you identify potential challenges and come up with solutions.

3. Network and Build Relationships: Real estate investing is a people business, and building relationships is essential for success. Attend networking events, join real estate investment clubs, and connect with other investors and professionals in the industry. These connections can help you find deals, get funding, and gain valuable advice and support.

4. Be Patient and Persistent: Real estate investing is not a get-rich-quick scheme. It takes time, effort, and persistence to achieve success. Be patient and persistent in your efforts, and do not give up if you encounter obstacles or setbacks. Learn from your mistakes and keep moving forward.

5. Focus on Cash Flow: Cash flow is the lifeblood of real estate investing. Focus on acquiring properties that generate

positive cash flow, rather than just looking for properties with potential appreciation. Positive cash flow can help you cover expenses, pay down debt, and reinvest in your business.

6. Manage Risk: Real estate investing involves risks, and it is important to manage them effectively. Conduct thorough due diligence before investing in a property, and have a contingency plan in case things do not go as planned. Consider using leverage, but do so wisely and within your means.

7. Have a Team of Professionals: Real estate investing involves various professionals, including real estate agents, attorneys, accountants, contractors, and property managers. Build a team of professionals who can help you navigate the complexities of the industry and provide expert advice and support.

8. Be Flexible and Adaptable: The real estate market is constantly changing, and it is important to be flexible and adaptable. Be open to new strategies, markets, and opportunities, and be willing to pivot when necessary. Keep an eye on market trends and adjust your business plan accordingly.

9. Treat Real Estate Investing as a Business: Real estate investing is a business, and it should be treated as such. Have a clear vision, mission, and set of core values. Establish standard operating procedures and systems, and monitor and measure your performance. Stay organized and keep detailed records of your investments.

10. Focus on Long-Term Wealth: Real estate investing is a powerful tool for building long-term wealth. Focus on acquiring properties that can provide steady cash flow and appreciation over the long term. Avoid making impulsive

decisions or chasing short-term gains at the expense of long-term success.

Conclusion:

The real estate market can be an excellent vehicle for building wealth and achieving financial independence. However, it requires knowledge, patience, persistence, and a willingness to take calculated risks. By following the tips outlined in this chapter, you can increase your chances of success in this exciting and rewarding industry. Remember to stay focused, stay informed, and stay committed to your goals.

In conclusion, real estate investment is a great way to generate long-term wealth and achieve financial freedom. However, it requires careful planning, research, and a deep understanding of the market. As a new investor, it's crucial to take the time to learn and understand the basics before making any investment decisions. Remember to diversify your portfolio, take advantage of tax benefits, and always have a contingency plan in case things don't go as expected. The real estate market can be unpredictable at times, but with the right approach, it can also be incredibly rewarding. Keep these tips in mind as you embark on your journey in real estate investment, and don't be afraid to seek guidance from experienced professionals along the way.

Made in the USA
Columbia, SC
18 January 2025